# The Untold Technique to
# Maximize Your Wealth

# The Untold Technique to Maximize Your Wealth

By David Podell

ISBN 978-1-300-26963-2

*Dedicated to my wife Danielle and daughter Tori*

# Table of Contents

# About the Author

David Podell has been in the financial planning industry for over ten years. He received his degree in finance from Hofstra University and continued his financial designations through the American College. He began his career as in intern with Merrill Lynch in 1997.

He is the current President of the Passaic/Bergen chapter of the National Association of Insurance and Financial Advisors.

He has been a Million Dollar Round Table "Top Of The Table" qualifier. This places Mr. Podell in the top 1% of all financial professionals, a career milestone attained only by those who have demonstrated exceptional professional knowledge, client service, and ethical conduct. Each year, only 3,500 people worldwide qualify for this.

He has qualified for Chairman Council status with New York Life and has conducted over thirty educational seminars on retirement income strategies.

He serves as a board member of the New Jersey Hofstra Alumni Association.

He founded his practice to bridge the divide between financial solutions and their purposes within an investment plan. He noticed early in his career that businesses and individuals were buying products that were not aligned with their goals. As an entrepreneur, he has developed a strong team to help people accumulate and protect their wealth.

David resides in New Jersey with his wife Danielle and daughter Tori. He enjoys golf, reading, working out, good food, and friends.

# Chapter 1

## The Role of Your Advisor

*The only way you can make your present better is by making your future bigger.*

*– Dan Sullivan*

*The greatest good you can do for another is not just to share your riches, but to reveal to him his own.*

*– Benjamin Disraeli*

I have gained experience a financial advisor over the years. I have seen many clients and thousands of financial situations. I want to share my knowledge and wisdom with open-minded people to help improve their lives and achieve their dreams. Contrary to what most people think, insurance and financial professionals are in the business of helping others. Our profession is sometimes viewed in a negative light due to the rare bad experience.

The relationship between a client and a financial advisor is one of trust—more than any other advisory relationship. A good financial professional yearns to develop a deep-rooted trust relationship. He partners with your genuine concerns and interest. He coordinates with your other advisors and quarterbacks all planning. He knows your hopes and dreams. My practice is focused on aligning our client's financial plan with their goals and vision.

Most people never achieve their vision because their portfolio consists of products that are not designed to work collectively. This requires comprehensive financial planning. Unfortunately, there are few advisors who take the time to do this type of planning. It is time consuming and tedious. But it allows us to get to know our client and the bond that gets developed is well worth the effort.

When you discuss your goals with your advisor, get specific. Retirement is not a goal. Spending six months a year in the sun, reading, skiing, and golfing, these are goals. These activities, along with any volunteer and charitable work, need dollar signs next to them. They must be factored into your planning. The advisor makes your life easier by guiding you through the jungle of potential solutions to the question, "How can I do all these things?"

If your advisor is not acting in this capacity, ask why. Find out if you are missing out on these services. If you are a "do-it-yourself" person, that is okay. There are those that want to take full control and make their own decisions. If you are diagnosing your own illnesses on WebMD, doing your taxes on TurboTax, or solving your estate tax issues on LegalZoom.com, I am not going to convince you to seek professional advice. But I do hope that this book will motivate you to take action on your own. I truly believe this untold technique will create wealth and abundance for your family and long-term future.

The concepts promoted in this book are not company specific. The principals are based on actual facts. We are not recommending any products or services. The main objective is for the reader to take action. That action should include meeting with their current advisor, or finding one that is a specialist in implementing these concepts. These methods are unique to the financial industry, but there are advisors who possess the knowledge and skill to incorporate these ideas into your personal planning. Any tax concepts should always be discussed with your own tax advisor.

# Chapter 2

## Asset Allocation Determines Your Investment Success

*Yesterday's home runs don't win today's games*

*- Babe Ruth*

We often talk about asset allocation as a pie with different pieces representing different sectors of the market. Let's look at this statistic. If you had invested (with all dividends reinvested) $100,000 divided proportionately between the weighted securities making up the Dow Jones Industrial Average on December 31, 1972, your balance on November 30, 1982, would have been $172,814. If you had allocated (with all dividends reinvested) your $100,000 with 60% in stocks, 30% in bonds, and 10% in cash using that same example, your account would have grown to $194,603. Each color in an asset allocation graphic represents a different sector of the market this could include: real estate, commodities, smaller companies, international companies, and many more. A well diversified portfolio exposes an investor to different areas of the market that could potentially do well, or not do so well. Over longer term time period, diversification and asset allocation are the key components to how you perform. When one investment category is down, another may be up.

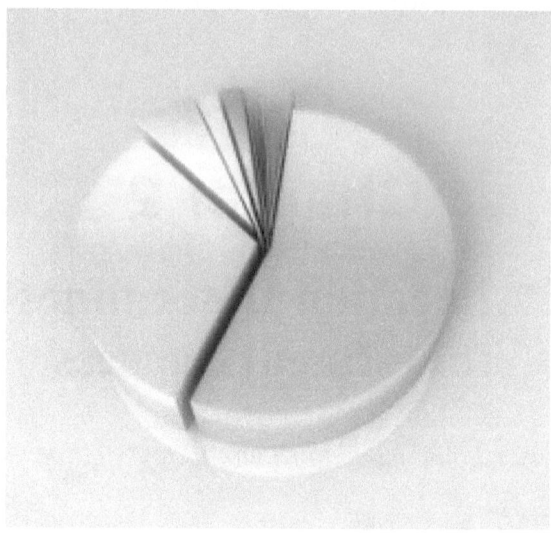

"Most people who invest are advised to diversify funds. This means taking one's total investments and dividing them into different groups. Overall, the goals we aim for when people diversify funds are that they will have both risk and profit shared among a large group of investments. In general, investment profiles that diversify funds have lower but more predictable returns.

"The old adage, 'Don't keep all your eggs in one basket,' applies to the fundamental principles of investment. If one invests in only one mutual fund, stock, or company, a loss means that the sole investment can be lost. However, when people diversify funds, a loss in one area may be made up for by gains in other areas. Thus all the 'eggs,' or in another words investments accumulated, are not lost.

"Generally when people diversify funds, they invest in three separate areas. A portion of the portfolio might include the purchase and ownership of stocks, bonds, and short-term investments. The risk when people diversify funds depends in part on what percentage of money is invested in each area."

As we get older, we often transfer riskier assets to safer investments. If half of the pie is in equity funds and the other half is in bond funds, an investor thinks they are "balanced." We were always told a percentage of your assets equal to your age should be invested in higher risk products. This means a thirty year old should have 30% safe and 70% in higher risk investments. The buy and hold/adjust as you get older strategy, however, is outmoded. The times have changed.

The buy and hold strategy is arguably deficient. Risk tolerance differs by individual investor. If you had $500,000 in your 401(k) and lost 37%, as most people did in 2008, your account value would have decreased to $315,000. Ask yourself, would you have re-allocated when you saw your account balance? Did you maintain your buy and hold strategy and make back all your money when the markets recovered?

## A Time-Tested Approach to Investing

According to a prominent study, 91.5% of the variance in an investment portfolio's return is due to asset allocation, while only 8.5% was attributed to other factors, such as security selection.[3]

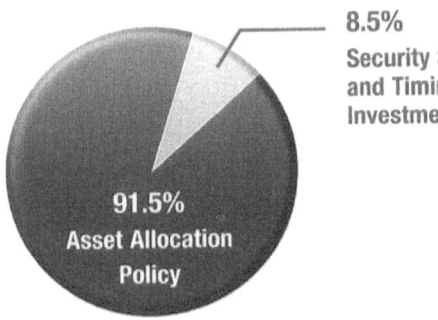

8.5%
Security Selection and Timing of Investments

91.5%
Asset Allocation Policy

# Chapter 3

## No One Seems to Be Saving Enough for Future Goals

*Life is not about waiting for the storm to pass; it's about dancing in the rain.*

*-- Anonymous*

Ask yourself, are you saving enough for your future goals? The answer nine out of ten times is no. That is because we as Americans like to spend and buy. This is great for the economy, but sometimes we want to purchase things that require excessive amounts of credit. This could be a more expensive home, college education, a high-priced car, a wedding, investment property, business venture, or simply a vacation that we have always dreamed about. Everyone has dreams that need funding. Forced savings vehicles are the paths to realizing those dreams. Cash value life insurance, investment portfolios, and bank accounts are all liquid vehicles that can be used to accumulate wealth and provide liquidity when the time comes.

Credit is readily available, and consumption is encouraged. We live in a world where instant gratification and material things give us pleasure and excitement. To quote Dorlan Francis, CLU, CFP, "The advent of life insurance with a reserve fund has proven to be the greatest financial innovation the world has known. Life insurance is not only the greatest mobilizer of savings, it thrives in an environment of low interest."

The reason for writing this book is simple. Permanent life insurance is by far the most underutilized financial tool in this country. I have seen those who plan properly experience so much prosperity, I believe it is my responsibility to demystify the misconceptions and share a concept that will improve the financial lives of others.

Most people are as changeable as the seasons in the way they treat their investments and savings. If the market is doing great and producing consistent returns, everyone talks about how well they are doing. The scarcity mentality disappears, and greed takes over. Everyone wants to jump on the boat. Emotions drive our actions; practicality and history are quickly forgotten. Our minds are trained to recover and move on. This holds true on the other side of the spectrum. When our portfolio loses 30%-50%, our anger tells us not to ever invest in the market again. We don't want to ever make the same mistake and lose money.

According to a study of the Dow Jones Industrial Average by American Funds Distributors, Inc., a leading mutual fund company, bear markets resulting in a decline of twenty percent or more occur about every 3.5 years. I have seen clients in real estate, equities, bond and credit markets, and business ventures react adversely to these market fluctuations. We all want our money to work for us, but emotion and fear can dominate our investment decisions. When the economy experiences instability in securities and the real estate markets, people reallocate their portfolios to overweight cash and non-productive vehicles like CD's, bonds, and money markets. This carries inflation risk and opportunity cost. Yes, you should invest in these vehicles, but they should remain a small piece of your total pie. They have a purpose; usually liquidity, emergency money, or segmentation to facilitate trading.

Permanent life insurance offers an alternative to emotional investing by providing a guaranteed death benefit for heirs in the event of an untimely death, as well as living benefits. A very tiny percentage of people actually do their own investing. Warren Buffett, John Paulson, and other professional money managers are among the few who can invest their wealth in their own funds. The majority of individuals and institutions invest money in an investment company; the managers of those institutions do the investing.

When we keep our money in the bank, we have no control over how the bank invests their assets. When we allocate our 401(k) fund, we have no control over what each fund does on a daily basis. We put our money in these vehicles and trust that the investment managers are going to continue to meet their historical rates of return.

Mutual insurance companies invest in products that the average investor cannot: cash and short term debt, government agencies, public investment grade debt, private investment deals, high-yield securities, commercial mortgage loans, private mortgage loans, real estate, and high quality equities. Approximately 85% of a mutual life insurer's portfolio is in fixed income with an "A" rated target rate, and the remainder is in equities. The portfolios are diversified, and unless you have billions of dollars to invest on your own, this portfolio holds hard-to-access investment products and reduced volatility.

# Chapter 4

## Life Insurance as an Asset Class

*The Wall Street Journal* July 28th 2012 ran an article titled, "Paying for College: Weighing Alternative Options." In the article, they highlight "permanent" life insurance as a method for parents to cover tuition bills using policy loans.[a] The article states, "Unlike 529 plans, Coverdell [Educations Savings] Accounts, and other vehicles, the asset value of a whole life insurance policy typically isn't included in calculations for financial aid eligibility."

By borrowing from these policies, parents are able to take cash value to cover tuition costs. Increased savings lead to a better quality of life that results in increased confidence and happiness. If you commit to a disciplined methodology of saving, you will be more in control of your financial life. Countries where people purchase more life insurance have statistically higher savings rates. Adequate savings are an essential part of economic prosperity. The majority of Americans will never save on their own. Business owners tend to keep too much equity in their businesses. Employees with retirement plans underfund these programs and do not align them with their personal financial plan.[2]

Modern Portfolio Theory (MPT), probably the most important economic theory, was developed in 1952 by Harry Markowitz and has influenced the greatest investors in the world. Markowitz shared a Nobel Prize in 1990 with Merton Miller and William Sharpe for what has become the most widely accepted method of portfolio selection, the idea of diversification in asset classes. When we say "asset classes," we are generally talking about equities or stocks, fixed income products or bonds, money markets or annuities, and real estate.

The theory was designed to offset systematic and unsystematic risk. Systematic risk includes a recession or interest rate changes. Unsystematic risk includes risk specific to individual stocks, businesses, or sectors of the economy.

Systematic planning is the main premise of the theory. I say systematic because it is a pro-active process that involves re-balancing, locking in gains, and, most important, proper diversification. I am passionate about this method because of the value it provides. Many financial plans have holes. Asset planning may not be as comprehensive as we often think. This system is designed to fill those holes and introduce a new way of thinking. I am so excited to share this idea because over the last few years more and more articles have appeared in which experts have supported this out-of-the-box concept. The idea has gained traction in the planning world. Of course one needs to keep in mind that no systematic plan of investing can protect fully against losses or guarantee a specific outcome.

The uncertainty of risk and reward can delay the development of a sound financial strategy. Life insurance is an ideal vehicle to integrate into Modern Portfolio Theory as an asset class of substantial value. From a retirement standpoint, everyone looks for income beyond social security. Life insurance is one vehicle that can add some degree of predictability to a portfolio. With the flexibility to strategically and actively manage portfolio allocation, your advisor can improve risk-adjusted returns. Most Americans rely on employer-sponsored plans, investments, and pensions for their retirement. The typical financial planner looks at life insurance as a necessary evil like automobile insurance. Any open-minded individual should ask the question, why would anyone want to own whole life insurance?

Randal Whittle nailed it on the head when he said it was "arguably the oldest, and therefore proven, financial instrument available in the toolbox. It has always worked through recessions and depressions and stock market crashes, wars, and upheaval. There hasn't been a single documented case in which it failed to work, or ever did anything to damage or cause loss to the owner. In good times it remains competitive, and generally carries tremendous tax-free growth benefits." [2]

Life insurance as an asset class has been used for years by the wealthy but has rarely been spoken about, in spite of its tremendous tax benefits. In the 2007 presidential campaign, John

McCain received campaign financing by using his three million dollar life insurance policy as collateral.

During the great depression, James Cash Penney was taken under the wing of the owners of a small store. They offered him a one-third partnership in a new store they were opening. During the next five years, James helped open two more stores and was doing very well. In 1912, he was running thirty-four stores in the Rocky Mountain region. He moved his company to Salt Lake City, Utah, and incorporated it under a name we all know today: the J.C Penney Company. The chain quickly grew to 1,400 stores by 1929. The stock market crashed, and the nation plunged into the Great Depression. The Depression destroyed his stores and wealth. But, because James had kept a safe foundation of money in his life insurance policies, he took out a loan on the accumulated cash value in his life insurance policy, and used it to meet his payroll and expenses for the entire chain. Not only did he keep his business, he flourished. Today, the stores take in revenues of $18.5 billion per year. Mr. Penney used a loan against his three million dollar policy to save his stores after the stock market crash.[2]

The story of Walt Disney says it all. In this case, one of the most popular animated characters was stolen by another studio. The top animator for the Disney Company left. They were in debt, and Walt Disney struggled for years on the brink of bankruptcy. In the 1950s, the only amusement parks in the entire country were dilapidated, with rusty, creaky rides and a reputation for unsanitary conditions. Walt dreamed of clean amusement parks filled with imaginative rides. He told investors about a place where families could make life-long memories, but no one believed it was possible. His brother Roy, his business partner and financial manager, said it couldn't be done. Determined to move ahead on his own, he applied for financing and was turned down by multiple banks. He emptied his savings account, sold his vacation home, and recruited a few employees who shared his vision. He used a loan from his cash value life insurance policies to help finance the park. On September 8, 1955, Disneyland opened with eighteen attractions. In the first month, it drew half a million visitors. By the end of the first year, it hosted more than 3.5 million guests. Less than three years later, it welcomed its ten millionth visitor—more than Yellowstone Park and the Grand Canyon.

You might have heard of a man named Ray Kroc who was working as a milkshake machine salesman in the 1950s. Being around hamburgers, he saw an opportunity and bought the rights to a burger stand in San Bernardino, California. In 1955, Ray opened the first McDonald's drive-in restaurant in Des Plaines, Illinois. He soon faced massive challenges with cash flow, franchises, competition, and the economy. He was determined to succeed and fought through it all. In order to get his company off the ground, he took out loans out against the cash value of his life insurance policies. He used this money to create an enduring advertising campaign that centered on the company's mascot, Ronald McDonald. In 1984, Ray passed away with 7,500 McDonald's restaurants operating worldwide. Today it has become the world's largest food service retailer in over sixty-five countries.

The country's largest banks invest much of their reserves into permanent life insurance due to its growth and safety. James Dyke wrote a detailed article in *Medical Economics* on this very issue. He stated that "a mix of term and permanent life insurance is ideal for most, though only permanent life offers interest rewards."

These ideas and facts have been written on and researched. It is exhilarating to see a message that I have believed in, come to the forefront of the industry. I do not expect everyone to agree on this, and I have therefore decided to address all counter arguments. This book is for those willing to forgo popular belief and examine nontraditional alternatives to accomplish some of your goals; life insurance which provides death benefit protection and access to cash value as emergency money for certain life events. Conventional financial planning works great in good times, but not in bad times. The invaluable tool of life insurance is a time-tested approach and will continue to grow and preserve wealth for years to come.

# Safety

*It's only when the tide goes out that you learn who's been swimming naked.*

*– Warren Buffet*

Just as we protect our cars, homes, and valuables, we need to protect our investments. When Wall Street firms went bankrupt in 2008 and the financial markets took a tumble, the winners who emerged had bet against the housing market. There is always someone on the other side of a trade. When you are selling, there is a buyer. If we don't provide a safe asset class that can stand the test of time, how else can we react when markets retract?

Life insurance is backed by the general account of a life insurance company. They must adhere to strict regulatory standards. In fact, most of these companies paid out dividends to their shareholders during this time.

I want to clarify the difference between "saving" and "investing." When one saves, money is safe and liquid. When one invests in a market that has ups and downs, your money can be at risk 100% of the time.

# Tax Benefits

*The only difference between the taxman and the taxidermist is that the taxidermist leaves the skin.*

*- Mark Twain*

The cash value of life insurance policies are tax-deferred, and loans are generally income tax-free and sometimes estate tax-free. If you dig into the financial statements of the ultra-wealthy, banks, and corporations, you may discover that these people own various permanent cash value life insurance policies. Rick Stivers, CFP, developed the Macro Asset Perspective around 2001 to illustrate how permanent life insurance would allow for more opportunities to accumulate wealth, by positioning your 401(k)'s and IRA's in an arena of higher risk in the early years, then more conservative risk later in life. The Macro Asset Perspective highlights the relationship between pre-tax and after-tax investments in conjunction with aggressive, moderate, and safe areas of one's financial picture. Diversification plays a key role here, and being on both sides of the tax fence allows you to keep more of the money you save for retirement.

Asset protection for business owners, medical professionals, and high-net-worth individuals is always a concern in this litigious country. Depending on where you live, life insurance policies can protect against bankruptcy and other legal proceedings. This asset is always accessible and can't be taken from you. Again, why wouldn't this be included in your portfolio?

Income tax-free death benefit: Even when you draw down your cash value, the policies can be structured to provide a death benefit to your beneficiaries regardless of how long you live.

Professional money management: Life Insurance company assets are professionally managed by some of the best managers in the industry. The portfolios are huge and aim to achieve the highest return with the maximum amount of safety.

A large part of financial planning is legacy planning. Life insurance can be assigned, accommodate complex beneficiaries, and can be changed without any legal documents. The beneficiaries will bypass probate and avoid appraisal costs, taxes, and other expenses that occur when one passes on.

Kim Butler describes the use of cash value life insurance as C.L.U.E

C= Control. Flow money to yourself in an account you control instead of away from yourself in accounts you don't control

L= Liquidity. Building wealth that cannot be taken from you by losses in the stock market or real estate downturns

U=Use. Saving money for later (retirement), or accessing it earlier for college needs, business opportunities, home improvements, etc.

E= Equity. Creating an account where you are benefiting from the ability to obtain a return that can be higher than your money sitting in bank accounts or cash equivalents.

# Chapter 5

# I Know What You're Thinking. Life Insurance, Come On…

*Do not expect the world to look bright, if you habitually wear gray-brown glasses.*

*– Charles William Eliot*
*(Longest-Serving president of Harvard University)*

To debunk any preconceived notions you have regarding the living benefits of life insurance, which are in addition to the death benefit protection, I want to address any negative sentiment with actual facts.

The most heard objection, is that you can do better investing all of your money in the stock market. This method is known as "buy term and invest the difference." Christopher R. Jarvis does a great job breaking this down in his article *Your Money: Bad Advice Debunked*. He says:

a) Many risky investments growing at 8% (taxable) are worth 5% to 6% (after taxes).

b) Accumulated cash-value in permanent life insurance policies are not taxed.

c) For relatively healthy individuals, the annualized cost of all internal expenses for cash-value life insurance is 1% to 2%.

d) For families in higher marginal tax brackets, premiums paid on an insurance policy can be less than the cost of taxes on a traditional market based investment.

Jarvis notes that without even factoring in the cost of term insurance (which would reduce the total amount in the mutual fund portfolio), a cash-value policy provided you need the death benefit first, may be a better alternative for many individuals who have this need.

The truth is, many people do need life insurance to pay for final expenses, estate and other taxes, or just to give you the ability to spend down your other retirement funds. If you believe that you will accumulate enough assets so that you will not need life insurance when your kids are older, or when you are retired, you are incorrect.

The more money you have, the more you need tax-efficient planning. Ignorance is a lack of knowledge or information. Sit down and look at your personal financial situation as soon as possible. Term is a cost that you might be able to reduce or eliminate by inserting that piece of the pie into its correct place. To quote Harold Evensky, a Miami financial planner, from a *New York Times* article: "I was a long-time believer in Term only, but now I believe that if someone will need insurance for ten years or longer, the tax advantage outweighs the advantage of buying term and investing the difference."[3]

He takes the example of a fifty-year-old healthy male who wants to invest $25,000 per year for fifteen years before retirement and then withdraw funds from age sixty-one to ninety. Assume the pre-tax earnings on both financial vehicles is 8% percent per year.

*     The person who invests in mutual funds withdraws $37,000 per year after taxes (without spending any money on term).

*     The person who purchased a cash-value life insurance withdraws a partial surrender value of $42,500 per year (paying no taxes on partial surrenders and loans) and has $1 million worth of life insurance protection.[2]

This is a simple example to reiterate the fact that permanent life insurance increases your returns and can be part of your investment portfolio because as the cash value accumulates; it becomes increasingly beneficial in overall risk reduction. Let's look at another example:

Richard Weber is a principal with The Ethical Edge, Inc., a Pleasant Hill, California, consulting firm. He co-authored a white paper that was commissioned by Guardian Life Insurance on life insurance as an asset class. He wrote, "Investment managers should realize there may be a place for life insurance as part of the fixed income part of a portfolio. Fixed income investments have low correlations to stocks. Life insurance cash values don't move in the same direction [as stocks or bonds] during a crisis."

One might feel life insurance should only be used for a death benefit. I urge you to put all your preconceived notions aside and consider looking at the living benefits in a permanent life insurance policy to accomplish some of your goals. Let's call it "icing on the cake". These methods are not meant to secure a legacy for your family. These provide living benefits to maximize your wealth.[h]

One might feel he or she is too old for the returns to make sense. Depending on one's age, insurance could be less effective in a portfolio. As you near retirement, adjust your allocations to reduce your risk and volatility. Using the potential accumulated cash value, growth is a long-term objective that can be accomplished. Depending on when you plan on retiring or withdrawing your cash value, it's still worth having an expert check all the numbers for you.

One might feel like he or she knows it all, and someone is trying to sell them a policy to earn a commission. For some reason, the media has touted these policies as high-commission products. Life insurance has commissions that are paid to the advisor who places the policies. Commissions are also paid on traditional investments such as: mutual funds, annuities, stocks, bonds, managed money, and all other financial instruments where there is an incentive offered to bring in assets. Financial service companies want to be profitable like any business. Advisor compensation should not be viewed negatively by the consumer if they are receiving value services for their money.

Brandon T. Roberts, Owner/Editor-in-Chief of *The Insurance Pro Blog*, frequently writes on this concept and has become its great advocate. A section of his December 2012 blog post is below:

*Let's take a look at an example to bring some concreteness to this whole idea. We'll take a man age 35 who plans to place $50,000 per year into a whole life policy.*

*If we take the traditional approach, some agent would simply specify the planned premium at $50,000 annually and solve for the corresponding death benefit. For the company I chose to run this example with, that comes out to $4,659,832.*

*We'll assume this individual is going to retire at age 65 and begin taking income from his whole life policy from age 66 to age 100 (most agents will assume something in the neighborhood of to age 80 because it'll show dramatically better income, I'm incredibly conservative so I build income scenarios that assume everyone lives at least to age 100).*

*At age 65 assumed cash value (the cash value based on the dividend) is $3,587,846, not too bad actually. By my math that's a 5.16% rate of return on a Compound Annual Growth Rate basis. Keep in mind tax-free. And it also already factors in all of those nasty insurance fees you'll hear about from the opposition. This will generate an assumed income from age 66 to 100 of $160,831.*

*The death benefit has grown to $7,626,233, that's a 9.13% annual rate of return, again tax-free when paid out at death.*

What if I can't pay my premium?

An insurance policy requires funding for a certain amount of time. If your life insurance asset class is being managed properly, it often makes sense to use profits from your risk-averse equities to pay premiums on your whole life policy. Sometimes an advisor will use bond yields to help build the cash position in the portfolio that is then used to pay the premiums. But there are many times when a portfolio is not producing returns, and it is not wise to pull money from the portfolio. In the meantime, premiums still need to be paid. After a few years of having a cash value policy, an automatic premium loan can be taken. This allows the policy owner to stop paying premiums out of their pocket. The premiums can be paid from the cash value account in the policy while enabling you to get dividends and growth.[a2]

Opportunity cost: One might feel that they are missing the opportunity to start a business, buy real estate, invest in an IPO, or any other opportunity that might come their way because they have tied up a significant piece of their current and future cash flow. Permanent insurance puts investors in a negative savings position in the early years. This is also the case with your mortgage. Does it make sense to have a mortgage, or to rent?[h] Term is renting your insurance and there is a 100% chance you will not recoup any money you put into your term policy unless you die in that specific time period. Therefore, the premium payments, which increase over time, are a pure expense. Permanent life insurance accumulates cash value and that affords living benefits in addition to death benefits.

I want to use a story that Kim Butler writes about in her book *Live Your Life Insurance: An Age-Old Approach Revitalized.*

In her book, she uses the story of John & Jane. John and Jane had wanted to open a toy store for years. He had a sales job, and she'd been home with the children while they researched various options. With a loan from the bank, they finally got started on their first store. It'd been open for about a year when an opportunity came along for a second store, but the bank wouldn't give them a second loan for the additional inventory. Their return on investment in the first store was over 20%, so they felt they could do the same in the new store if they could just get the inventory. They'd been faithfully funding their life insurance for seven years and were surprised to learn how quickly and easily they could borrow against its cash value. They opened their second store and began paying back the life insurance loan from the sales right away (since it was summer and sales were high). After Christmas, sales were slow. They took a break from the payments and then resumed them again the next summer. After three summers of diligent loan payments, the loan against the cash value was paid off, and they were able to use the cash value again for another investment.

Stephen Horan, Ph.D., CFA, head of private wealth management at the CFA Institute in Charlottesville, Virginia, has no business ties to the insurance industry. He notes that defining an asset class is as much art as science. Horan believes life insurance should be considered its own asset class. "From a deconstructionist standpoint, an asset is something that generates an expected future cash flow either in the form of income or capital gain and that can be financial, (or) it can be physical," he says. "Life insurance fits that profile."

# Chapter 6

## Life Insurance <u>in</u> a Portfolio versus Life Insurance <u>not</u> in a Portfolio

Weber's studies compared an existing portfolio <u>with</u> permanent life insurance as an asset class. The portfolio with permanent life insurance outperformed the portfolio <u>without</u> life insurance and had less risk.

In this case, the study took a forty-five-year-old male with $500,000 invested in municipal bonds and assumed the bonds grew at a 4% annual rate. The investment was worth $2.9 million by the time the male was age eighty-nine.

Next, they assumed that instead of reinvesting the $20,000 of the initial municipal bond income, the money was used to buy a permanent whole life policy. After the first nineteen years, the bonds and cash value portfolios outperformed the municipal bond portfolio. By the time the male was eighty-nine years old, the bonds and cash value portfolio had a value of $3.5 million! This was a result of the cash value allowing for more risk with the traditional asset classes in the portfolio.

In this example, before the first nineteen years, the bonds only portfolio asset value was slightly higher than the life insurance, but less liquid and higher risk.

The bond portfolio that included cash-value life insurance was less risky. It grew at 4.77% with a risk measure of 2.09. The bond portfolio without any life insurance grew at a 4% annual rate with a higher risk of 2.48.

A white paper that was published by Richard L. Miller, CLU, ChFC, titled, "The Truth About Participating Whole Life: Is Whole Life an Obsolete Product?" An actual case based on the last 49 years, provides the surprising answer using data from a policy that was issued in 1963. The updates occurred every June and included numbers from a policy that had been in force for the prior forty-nine years. The author has continued to update it every year since he originally published the article back in 2009. Mr. Miller's paper has real numbers that alone warrant taking the time to read it. The actual facts he provides are very impressive. He compares his guaranteed cash value and his paid up additions/dividends to what he would have gotten using a bank cd and investing in term. The permanent life insurance policy is significantly higher over this time period. This is not a comparison he is showing to investing in the market, but rather to controlling the cash in the policy vs. an alternative safe vehicle. CD's have had years since 1963 of very high interest rates, and some lower interest rate years. To conclude the study, his whole life policy has withstood consistent growth over 49 years.[g]

From the years 2000 to 2010, many permanent policies produced rates of return that were four to five times that of the S&P 500 index. As I have previously stated, this is not meant to be used as your full financial plan. Investors tend to make changes and trades based on emotion and are very reactive. Whether your portfolio is passive in a 401(k) plan or active in a managed account, this approach will bring consistency to your overall plan.

Another example below includes two allocations that might sometimes be suitable for a moderate growth portfolio. Both contain 27% in fixed income and 73% in equities. By placing 20% of the portfolio assets in cash value life insurance,

a)    the expected return increased from 8.35% to 8.65%;

b)    the standard deviation (standard deviation is also known as historical volatility and is used by investors as a gauge for the amount of expected volatility) decreased from 14.38% to 13.62% ;[x]

c)    the median expected value in thirty years rose from $2,449,000 to $2,748,000 (a $299,000 increase).

### Portfolio A: Without Life Insurance Cash Value

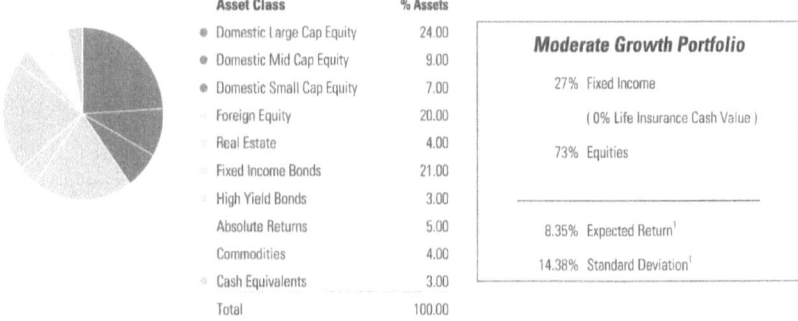

| Asset Class | % Assets |
|---|---|
| ● Domestic Large Cap Equity | 24.00 |
| ● Domestic Mid Cap Equity | 9.00 |
| ● Domestic Small Cap Equity | 7.00 |
| Foreign Equity | 20.00 |
| Real Estate | 4.00 |
| Fixed Income Bonds | 21.00 |
| High Yield Bonds | 3.00 |
| Absolute Returns | 5.00 |
| Commodities | 4.00 |
| Cash Equivalents | 3.00 |
| Total | 100.00 |

**Moderate Growth Portfolio**

27%  Fixed Income
    ( 0% Life Insurance Cash Value )

73%  Equities

-----

8.35%  Expected Return[1]
14.38%  Standard Deviation[1]

### Portfolio B: With Life Insurance Cash Value

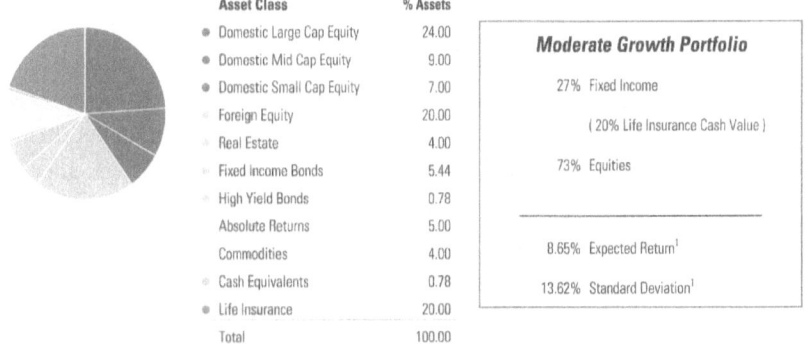

| Asset Class | % Assets |
|---|---|
| ● Domestic Large Cap Equity | 24.00 |
| ● Domestic Mid Cap Equity | 9.00 |
| ● Domestic Small Cap Equity | 7.00 |
| Foreign Equity | 20.00 |
| Real Estate | 4.00 |
| Fixed Income Bonds | 5.44 |
| High Yield Bonds | 0.78 |
| Absolute Returns | 5.00 |
| Commodities | 4.00 |
| Cash Equivalents | 0.78 |
| ● Life Insurance | 20.00 |
| Total | 100.00 |

**Moderate Growth Portfolio**

27%  Fixed Income
    ( 20% Life Insurance Cash Value )

73%  Equities

-----

8.65%  Expected Return[1]
13.62%  Standard Deviation[1]

[1] Estimating Expected Return and Standard Deviation of New York Life Insurance Company General Account for Investors, Ibbotson Associates, 2009. Figures have been rounded to the nearest tenth of a percent.

According to another independent study by Ibbotson Associates, when a portfolio is diversified to include cash value life insurance, it can produce higher expected returns and a lower standard deviation (risk) than a portfolio without life insurance. When Ibbotson conducted this study, they measured the expected returns and standard deviation of sample portfolios. Ibbotson mathematically replaced a portion of the portfolio's traditional fixed income investments with a cash value life insurance policy.

This was done with a moderate investment portfolio that had 54% in fixed income and 46% in equities.

* Portfolio A contained traditional fixed income asset classes such as High Yield Bonds, TIPS(Treasury Inflation-Protected Securities), Short Term Bonds, and Cash Equivalents with an expected annual rate of return of 8.35%.

* Portfolio B contained these same asset classes, but allocated a portion of the investment in fixed income products to Life Insurance Cash Value, with an expected annual rate of return of 8.65%.[x]

*The sad Truth of the matter is that over time the vast majority—approximately 80 percent—of the mutual funds underperform the overall stock market.*

*- The Motley Fool*

Paul Sullivan from *The New York Times* wrote that "some financial advisors have begun encouraging clients to buy permanent life insurance—permanent because it does not lapse,[j] like term insurance, after a set time—as a substitute for bonds in their portfolio. Their argument is threefold: the rate of return on permanent life insurance can be three to five percent, the money in a permanent policy generally passes to beneficiaries free of income tax, and owners can borrow against the policy without incurring any taxes. If they do not repay the loan, it will simply be deducted from the death benefit."[ja2]

In the article, Paul quoted Bob Plybon, chief executive of Plybon & Associates, a wealth advisor in Greensboro, North Carolina. "I think where we are from an economic standpoint, it makes tremendous sense to look at it as an asset class. Right now, you have the ability to generate yields that are competitive with other investments." He also interviewed Adam Sherman, chief executive of Firstrust Financial Resources, a wealth manager and insurance broker in Philadelphia. "Given how the world looks, is it bad to have a five percent tool in your investment box? It's not going to hurt you."

Mr. Plybon described a case where a couple in their 70s wanted to buy a large policy after their net worth was reduced from

$30 million to $20 million in 2008. The couple wanted a way to get back their net worth because they had earmarked it for a foundation. They paid a premium of one million dollars to secure a policy that would pay out $10 million after both of them died. When asked why not just invest the money in other faster-growing assets, they responded, "They didn't want to take a chance." Mr. Plybon said, "They wanted to get less aggressive, not more aggressive."

Leslie Scism of the *Wall Street Journal* recently wrote an article where she noted, "Many small investors, feeling burned by the financial markets, are using permanent-life policies in place of other investments.ˆ George Carapella, a tax preparer in Staten Island, N.Y., soured on stocks and funds after the tech-stock and housing bubbles burst. The investments 'didn't work out,' the 53 year-old says. 'Too many crashes. I said, Who am I kidding?' Instead he bought a $500,000 whole life policy from National Life Group a policyholder-owned insurer in Montpelier, VT. Mr. Carapella says he likes that the insurer invests the money in bonds and real estate."

There are only a few solid requests that clients have when they come to us to discuss their investments.

1)    Those looking to accumulate assets want to achieve as much possible gain while reducing their risk and fluctuation.

2)    They want us to communicate with them when we feel an adjustment needs to be made in their portfolio.

3)    They want to know that they are moving in the right direction and are not missing out on any opportunities.

The concept of using cash value life insurance as a component in a portfolio was developed from a study done by Ibbotson and Morningstar, two independent companies, on a major insurer's general account, which maintains over $150 billion in assets. These two companies went back to 1982 to determine the risk and return characteristics of a major life insurer's general account. The study showed that by including the cash value from a life insurance policy as a portion of fixed income, the overall investment portfolio return would be increased with less risk. The efficient frontier line represents where risk is minimized for each rate of return, and where the return is maximized for each degree of risk. If a portfolio falls along the efficient frontier, it is an optimized portfolio. The difference between the two portfolios can be significant. Whole life insurance has a benefit of tax-deferred cash value accumulation and the opportunity to earn dividends if the company declares them. The ability to borrow from the cash value is generally on a tax-free basis (loans accrue interest and reduce the cash value and death benefit).

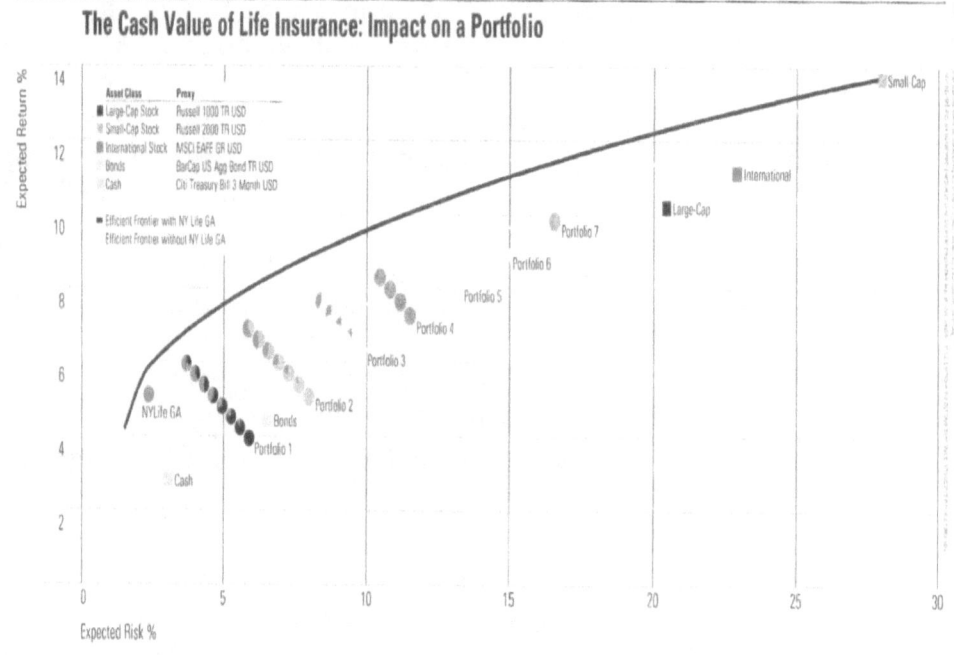

Chart details ᵥ

If you are wondering why you haven't heard of this before, it is because many advisors do not have expertise for this specific concept. This is a unique concept and gives many advisors a competitive advantage in the marketplace. This is about stepping out of the box and showing ordinary people nontraditional ways to create and build capital the same way our high-net-worth clients do.

Go to any bank and ask for a loan application. Tell them you are buying a business, house, boat, or apartment building. The bank is going to hand you an application and financial statement. The financial statement is going to ask how much cash value is in your life insurance. If you currently only have term, you must answer zero. If you can follow the concepts in this book, at some point you should be able to list a number that may be sizable, and the bank will look more favorably on your loan application. You have shown that you have a safe asset that you can tap into via loans, and that in most states are protected from creditors and are growing in a tax-deferred way. Banks and lenders view our credit reports as a symbol of our financial trustworthiness, and our capital assets play the same role.

# Chapter 7

## Using This Technique with Your 401(k) or Retirement Plan

Most 401(k), IRA's, and 403(b) plans are invested in mutual fund options. Mutual funds control a major portion of all savings in the United States. If you are an employee of a company with one of these plans, you know a portion of your check can automatically be swept into one of these types of accounts. We usually do not think that we can lose 100% of our account value. It takes some really down years in the market for the fear to become a reality. When this reality hits us, the average investor starts moving their funds around. Emotion takes over, and we make irrational financial decisions. When the market recovers, we then forget about the losses and try to chase back the returns we hear our colleagues boasting about.

In recent years, the industry has made it easier to contribute a large portion of our paychecks to these plans. Products now include mutual funds called lifestyle or target date funds. The employer rarely looks at the cost to employees, because it comes out of *your* return, not your company's. Unlike taxable investments, which are liquid, assets locked up in a 401(k), IRA, or 403(b) have restrictions, should you want to withdraw funds below the retirement age.

When we choose asset classes in our retirement plans, we usually choose a few different funds based on their level of risk. Most investors look at returns to determine what did well and how much they should allocate to those asset classes. What isn't usually considered is that an asset class that returned 38% last year could actually return -38% this year. So how do we make educated choices? We have to look at macro views and actual facts.

Remember, asset allocation is a huge part of managing how your portfolio will perform.

## Taking Turns at the Top

Annual Total Returns for Key Asset Classes – Ranked in Order of Performance

Chart showing annual total returns for key asset classes from 1995 to 2011, ranked from Best (top) to Worst (bottom).

Legend:

- Categories Blended Return.
- Bonds are represented by the Barclays Capital Aggregate Bond Index.
- Large stocks are represented by the S&P 500 Index.
- Large growth stocks are represented by the Russell 1000 Growth Index.
- Large value stocks are represented by the Russell 1000 Value Index.
- Midcap stocks are represented by the Russell MidCap Index.
- Midcap growth stocks are represented by the Russell MidCap Growth Index.
- Midcap value stocks are represented by the Russell MidCap Value Index.
- Foreign stocks are represented by the MSCI EAFE Index.
- Small stocks are represented by the Russell 2000 Index.
- Small growth stocks are represented by the Russell 2000 Growth Index.
- Small value stocks are represented by the Russell 2000 Value Index.
- Floating rate loans are represented by the Credit Suisse Leveraged Loan Index.

You can try to look for a pattern in the chart above, but you will always find this phrase in every prospectus: *Past performance is no indication of future results.* And this is true. Small value funds looked great in 2000 and 2001, but those gains were most likely erased if you held on in 2002, 2008, and 2011.

Let's take a look at more facts. Joe is age 32 and puts $1,000/month away into a life insurance policy but he wanted to use this money for certain emergencies, living benefits, or to supplement his retirement income. He also wanted to be able to tap into it for his kids college education. We designed a strategy using a permanent whole life insurance policy to help him accomplish his goals:

1)  He is finished paying premiums at age 47 guaranteed.

2)  At age 47 he is able to withdrawal $18,000/year for each of his children to attend college for all years until both are out of school, and Joe is now age 53. (Even though they overlap years while going to college, he is still is able to take out $126,000 for total education expenses.

3)  At age 65 Joe is able to withdraw $25,000/year for his first 10 years in retirement.

4)  Joe paid a total of $168,000 in premiums. He took out $126,000 for education expenses and $250,000 for retirement. He pays ZERO taxes, and has death benefit to still leave his family for the rest of his life, as an added benefit.[d]

The argument here is that Joe could have less money than his 401k would provide for retirement income. That is absolutely true. This financial vehicle doesn't have market risk. This is a conservative way to build cash value for living benefits and still provide a legacy for your loved ones. It works amazingly well in conjunction with a qualified retirement plan. This is also the reason that life insurance is an asset class that should be used as a piece of the pie rather than the entire pie.

Insurance policies can be designed well if you are thirty-two or fifty-two. Everyone has a different need and situation. It is important to use an advisor who has experience in this type of planning.

What type of insurance should be used for this strategy?

Life insurance is a very complex planning tool. Each person is different, and your needs must be assessed by your financial advisor. This strategy requires some form of whole life insurance designed specifically to collaborate with your other investments to accomplish certain goals. The policy needs to be put together for accumulation and protection of investment gains.[h] This can be accomplished by partially converting term insurance over a period of years or shifting assets one-time into a properly-designed policy. It is imperative to choose a company that has a sound financial history and is highly rated. Dividend growth potential is a key factor in how much your cash value can increase.

The recent stock market collapse was devastating to so many individual holdings because it affected both equities and bonds,

People who thought their portfolios were adequately diversified across stocks, bonds, and traditional fixed assets still saw significant losses in their 401(k)'s.

Whole life was one of the few financial assets that did not lose value because it is not tied to market performance; indeed, many policyholders found that it was the only statement they looked forward to opening over the past year.

Financial industry consultants Richard M. Weber, MBA, CLU, AEP, and Christopher Hause, FSA, MAAA, first introduced the concept underlying Life Insurance as an Asset Class, in an Academy of Financial Services Best Paper 2008. Grounded in classic Modern Portfolio Theory, Weber and Hause were able to document the conclusion that whole life insurance provides unexpectedly solid performance at relatively low risk. As a complement to other fixed-income assets, they found that whole life provides:

- Guaranteed protection to help increase future predictability in a portfolio;
- Attractive tax advantages; and, perhaps most important to skittish investors,
- Guaranteed growth disassociated from market volatility.

The following graphs are intended to illustrate a sample of the individual test trials produced for your portfolios based on the projected rates of return and standard deviation over a 30 year time horizon. The graphs depict the $5^{th}$, $25^{th}$, $50^{th}$ (Median Result), $75^{th}$ and $90^{th}$ percentiles. These results are based on 500 separate trials. Rates of return and standard deviations have been rounded to the nearest tenth of a percent. Expected portfolio values have been rounded to the nearest ten thousand.

**How to Interpret the Analysis:** Each percentile represents a greater probability that your portfolio will be able to produce the expected return. For example, in Portfolio A, the $25^{th}$ percentile has an ending value of approximately $4,210,000. This means that 25% of the time, if the funds remained invested in this portfolio for 30 years, they would be expected to have a value of $4,210,000 or more. Portfolio value at inception is 300K.

### Portfolio A: Without Life Insurance Cash Value

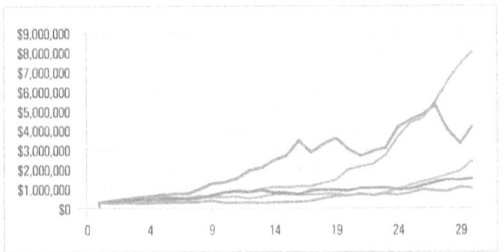

### Portfolio B: With Life Insurance Cash Value[1]

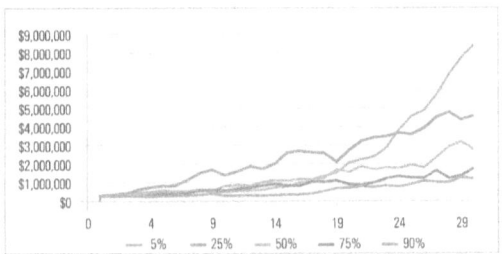

— 5%   — 25%   — 50%   — 75%   — 90%

| | Expected Rate of Return | Standard Deviation | 5% of outcomes greater than | 25% of outcomes greater than | 50% of outcomes greater than | 75% of outcomes greater than | 90% of outcomes greater than |
|---|---|---|---|---|---|---|---|
| Portfolio A 0% Life Insurance Cash Value | 8.35% | 14.38% | $8,040,000 | $4,210,000 | $2,449,000 | $1,520,000 | $1,020,000 |
| Portfolio B 20% Life Insurance Cash Value | 8.65% | 13.62% | $8,420,000 | $4,590,000 | $2,748,000 | $1,760,000 | $1,200,000 |
| Expected Change $ | | | $380,000 | $380,000 | $299,000 | $240,000 | $180,000 |
| Expected Change % | 0.30% | -0.76% | 5% | 9% | 12% | 16% | 18% |

[1]Chart results are derived from Ibbotson Associates' assumptions on rates of return and standard deviations of a moderate growth portfolio with a 20% allocation to life insurance cash value. See disclosure pages for additional information.

*Rates of return and standard deviations have been rounded to the nearest tenth of a percent. Expected portfolio values have been rounded to the nearest hundred thousand. Loans against your policy accrue interest at the current variable loan interest and decrease the death benefit and cash value by the amount of the outstanding loan and loan interest. Hypothetical illustration based on expected return and standard deviation of model portfolios with and without life insurance cash value incorporated as part of fixed income asset class.$_x$*

Cash Value Life Insurance should be actively managed like any other asset class.

We need to look ahead and ask questions earlier. What happens in retirement? How do distributions work? Typically retirees only want to spend what they must, and leave an estate or inheritance to their children and grandchildren. Using this concept, you actually have a death benefit that, if managed correctly, will leave an inheritance to your children. The best part about this is that you are able to take cash out of the policy during your lifetime: loans, your basis, and dividends. Depending on how much of an inheritance you want to leave, using your existing policy might or might not be enough. You have put yourself in a situation that allows you to spend down your assets in retirement and live on more income that is tax-free.

One of the current experts on monetary and banking theory, economist Huerta de Soto, writes:

"The institution of life insurance has gradually and spontaneously taken shape in the market over the last two hundred years. It is based on a series of technical, actuarial, financial and juridical principals of business behavior which have enabled it to perform its mission perfectly and survive economic crises and recessions which other institutions, especially banking, have been unable to overcome. Therefore the high 'financial death rate' of banks, which systematically suspend payments and fail without the support of the central bank, has historically contrasted with the health and technical solvency of life insurance companies. (In the last two hundred years, a negligible number of life insurance companies have disappeared due to financial difficulties.)" – Jesus Huerta De Soto, *Money, Bank Credit, and Economic Cycles* (Auburn, AL: The Ludwig von Mises Institute, 2009), p.590.

# Chapter 8

## Make It Happen

*People of accomplishment rarely sat back & let things happen to them. They went out & happened to things.*

*--Leonardo Da Vinci*

We all save for our later years for various reasons, sometimes for leisure activities we do not currently have time for and sometimes to provide enough assets to fully retire. When income stops or slows down, your financial goals shift. You enter a distribution stage. This stage requires financial planning and professional advice that focuses on how you should be taking your money out of all financial instruments. The accumulated cash value in permanent life insurance can be turned into income or an annuity, or you might want to have the flexibility to take out a portion of your accumulated cash value, in whatever amounts you wish, each year.

By using life insurance as an asset class, you are able to maximize your returns over the years with riskier investments (due to the added source of fixed income), and now have to consider age, guaranteed and discretionary income needs, legacy needs, and an optimal withdrawal rate from your portfolio. Your tax situation should be assessed by your tax advisor. Your estate should be updated to reflect current laws and changes. These are all planning issues about which thousands of books and articles have been written. By gaining a better understanding on some of the options we discussed in this book, you can position your finances to plan for what you want for your own retirement. Other methods often lack predictability, and fail.

To reiterate, the goal here is to open your mind to a strategy that is being used by high-net-worth individuals and could work for you. This is the same strategy that can be used by any ordinary saver if structured properly. I highly recommend you meet with a financial planner who has the expertise and experience in this area. If your advisor does not specialize in this, look for someone that does, but make sure they are going to rebalance your portfolio in coordination with this asset class. You could be reading this book during a time of high interest rates or a robust stock market. If so, the thought of putting significant contributions into a vehicle that produces a lower return, will seem like lost opportunity. It's important to think about the future and realize that what goes up, always comes down. This thesis applies to big picture long term wealth, not short term gains. Wayne Gretzky once said "I skate to where the puck is going to be, not where it has been." Human nature has us chasing returns and opportunities that are already on the surface, when we should be thinking about what the future may hold.

The relationship you develop with your advisor managing this type of asset must be long-term and cannot be just a sales transaction. The concept will not work. If you are worried about having less of a death benefit when you draw on your money, you should discuss the option of having a term policy to supplement your insurance needs. Life insurance leaves a legacy to your family. This strategy is first and foremost for the person who wants to amass wealth over the long run. This idea has not been publicized enough, and I hope you will investigate how you can personally benefit from it. My objective is to drastically improve the financial lives of my clients. Lee Brower, a great estate planner and author said "The best season of your life lies ahead. No matter what your age or station in life–you have a choice. Ninety percent of your potential is not only untapped and unused, but also undiscovered."

I hope this book will get you to take the first step to tap the untold technique of maximizing your own wealth.

*Million dollar ideas are a dime a dozen. The determination to see the idea through is what's priceless.*

*-Robert Dieffenbach*

# Acknowledgements

**George Yackulic**. The largest benefactor of my success who brought me into the business and always encouraged me to achieve way beyond the average advisor.

**MY CLIENTS**. They have placed tremendous trust in me to educate them to plan their lives and make the right decisions. We have done this to provide a financial path to prosperity and security for their families' future. It is this high-level trust that has allowed them to act upon our strategies and recommendations. These relationships are sacred, and I wouldn't be where I am without them.

**Strategic Coach.** For forcing me to think outside the box and grow my practice as an entrepreneur that truly delivers a competitive advantage to the marketplace. Since we started using the strategic coach practice management tools, our practice has grown tremendously.

**MY TEAM** – who works hard every day to collectively make sure we are doing the very best for our clients, and support my overall vision.

# Notes and Disclosures

This book is not intended to provide any tax or legal advice as we do not have the expertise to recommend it.

New York Life Investments is a service mark used by New York Life Investment Management Holdings LLC and its subsidiary, New York Life Investment Management LLC.

(1) Source: Pensions & Investments, May 31, 2010.

Barry James Dyke wrote the June 19, 2009 Medical Economics article *New Life for Life Insurance.*

Christopher R. Jarvis, MBA. *Physicians Practice Magazine.*

*Life Insurance as an Asset Class*. April 19, 2011, by Alan Lavine - quoted Richard Weber and Christopher Hause.

*Walt Disney, McDonald's and Using Celebrities to Kill Life Insurance Objections* by Brett K, Insurance Mavericks from 8/17/11 producersweb.com.

Adapted from Catherine and Richard Greene, *The Man Behind the Magic: The Story of Walt Disney* (NY: Viking Penguin, 1991)

*Wall Street Journal*. Saturday/Sunday July 28-29, 2012. *Paying for College: Weighing Alternative Options* written by AnnaMaria Andriotis.

*Live Your Life Insurance: An Age-Old Approach Revitalized* by Kim Butler and Randal Whittle.

*Life Insurance: The Cause of Economic Prosperity* by Dorlan H. Francis CLU, CFP.

*The Perfect Non-Correlated Asset*. Brian Ashe, CLU, Brian Ashe and Associates. NAIFA Article May/June 2012.

*Wall Street Journal* article by Leslie Scism, *Life Policies: The Whole Truth* appeared in the Saturday/Sunday, June 9-10, 2012.

Ike Devji, J.D. *How Physicians Can Stop Hating Life Insurance (Part I and Part II)*. July 26, 2011 and August 2, 2011.

*Viewing Life Insurance as an Asset Class* by Ed McCarthy, CFP, August 27, 2012 from AdvisorOne article online on 9/3/2012.

**We Still Beat the Cash Value Life Insurance Drum** by Brantley Whitley on Friday, November 9, 2012 | No Comments http://theinsuranceproblog.com/still-beating-the-cash-value-life-insurance-drum/

[a] Loans accrue interest and lower the death benefit if not paid back.

[2] Please note that access to cash value via a loan will accrue interest and if not paid back will lower the death benefit

[3] This may be true for many people who have the life insurance need and can afford to buy a permanent life insurance policy.

[h] This will depend on each individuals needs and financial situation.  This is totally dependent on what your personal primary goal would be. Death Benefit is the primary purpose of life insurance and cash values are secondary

[j] provided that one continues to pay their premiums

[^]So they can preserve a legacy for their loved ones

[v]What is efficient frontier? – it is represented by the lines in the graph as the best trade-off between rish(standard deviation) and the expected return.  Investors stive for a portfolio that is as close toto the efficient frontier as possible.  We know that inorder to achieve higher expected return an investor must take on more risk.  This concept is illustrated by the upward-sloping line in the graph above.

Where do the Lifetime Wealth Portfolios fit in?
The asset allocation of the Lifetime Wealth Portfolios was
developed by Ibbotson Associates and is used as the basis for each
portfolio that Ibbotson and Morningstar Investment Services offer.
These allocations are plotted in the graph above along with the
relevant benchmarks.  Also included is the New York Life
Insurance General Account, represented in the graph as "NYLIFE
GA."  The dark line represents the efficient frontier with the
General Account; the gray line, without.  Ibbotson has reviewed
the New York Life Insurance Company General Account and
estimated the expected return and standard deviation for this
account using re-sampling and sensitivity analysis.  This helps to
build more robust portfolios and to ensure stability in a variety of
market scenarios, resulting in portfolios that are slightly below the
efficient frontier line.

What is the impact of the cash value of life insurance on my
portfolio?  You'll notice that for Portfolios 1,2, and 3, there is a
track leading closer to the efficient frontier, representing the
changes in the portfolio as the cash value of life insurance is
incorporated.  This is show in 10% increments, moving the
portfolio progressively closer to the efficient frontier.

$_x$The expected return and standard deviation for insurance products
used in this study are estimated based on a model portfolio
constructed to approximate the gross asset class returns within the
underlying investment portfolio associated with New York Life
Whole life insurance policies.  For these analysis's, gross returns
are used ignoring expenses and mortality costs which will vary
based upon your age, underwriting risk classification, and the
number of years you hold the policy.  The Analysis assumes you
will hold the policy for 30 year and it reflects long-term
performance.  In the early years, where significant cash value has
not yet accumulated, internal rates of return on cash value will be
lower.  You should consult your insurance agent and review a
complete illustration for the policy you are considering before
making an insurance purchase decision.  This analysis does not
suggest the actual outcome of any specific New York Life product

or imply that a personal investment into New York Life's general account is possible.

Walt Disney, McDonald's and using celebrities to kill life insurance objectives by Brett K, Insurance Mavericks – 8/17/2011. www.producerweb.com/r/pwebmc/d

[d] This was taken from a New York Life sample illustration that was ran on 10/31/2011. These are non-guaranteed figures based on dividends and was ran as a non-smoker. This is neither an estimate nor guarantee of future performance. Taking cash out will reduce your death benefit. This illustration should in no way be used to compare to your personal situation.

[g] For illustrative purposes only. Individual results will vary. The example is for a specific whole life policy for a specific medical class and age and should not be taken on guaranteed purposes. It is only specific to this actual person. Other rate classes are available. Life insurance application is subject to underwriting.

[χ] Expected return figures do not include expenses or mortality costs. Actual returns will be reduced by fees and other expenses and are dependent in part on dividends declared by the issuing company. The expected return and standard deviation for insurance products used in the study are estimated based on a model portfolio constructed to approximate the gross asset class returns within the underlying investment portfolio associated with New York Life whole life insurance policies.

For this analysis, gross returns are used ignoring expenses and mortality costs, which will vary based upon age, underwriting risk classification, and the number of years the policy is held. The analysis assumes policy owner will hold the policy for 30 years, and it reflects probable long-term performance. In early years, where significant cash value has not yet accumulated, internal rates of return on cash value will be lower.

There can be no assurances that any financial strategy will be successful. Actual results will vary based upon their individual situation and the actual performance of any products or investments they ultimately decide to purchase.

Clients should review a complete illustration for the policy they are considering before making an insurance purchase decision. This analysis does not suggest the actual outcome of any specific New York Life product or imply that a personal investment into New York Life's general account is possible.

The content in this book is meant for general information and education purposes only. It is mostly based on the author's work experience, as well as information that have been gathered from various sources, which are believed to be reliable. However, the author makes no representation as to the accuracy of this third party content. The content of this book is not intended to be an offer or a recommendation of any specific financial or insurance products or services discussed. It is not meant as financial, tax or insurance advice, which must all be coordinated based on the individual's specific situation. If you wish to consider any of the strategies discussed in this book please be sure to consult with your own personal adviser or a professional focused in these areas. Any examples discussed and illustrated scenarios are hypothetical and are not representative of actual results on any specific insurance or financial products which would need to be based on an individual's specific situation and needs. When purchasing any life insurance policy, please note that you must be provided a full basic illustration specific to you on the insurance policy or policies you are considering.

www.ingramcontent.com/pod-product-compliance
Lightning Source LLC
Chambersburg PA
CBHW021927170526
45157CB00005B/2216